Lundgren, Julie K.

Grassland buffet:
studying food webs in the
grasslands and savannahs

STUDYING FOOD WEBS

GRASSLAND BUFFET

Studying Food Webs in the Grasslands and Savannas

JULIE K. LUNDGREN

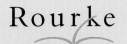

Rourke
Publishing LLC
Vero Beach, Florida 32964

www.rourkepublishing.com

Project Assistance:
Also, the author thanks Sam Lundgren, Tracy Nelson Maurer and the team at Blue Door Publishing.

Photo credits: Cover Images - landscape © pmphoto, wolf © Eric Lawton, bison © Ken Canning, sun © Galyna Andrushko, grass © Ken Canning; Pages 4, 5 ©Victor Soares, Page 5 © Galyna Andrushko, Hywit Dimyadi; Page 6 © Maxim Pushkarev, Weldon Schloneger; Page 7 © José, eismcsquare; Page 8 © Galyna Andrushko; Page 9 © ANP, Dark O; Page 10 © TeunSpaans; Page 10b - US Environmental Protection Agency; Page 11 © ZTS; Page 12 © Eric Gevaert; Page 13 © Steffen Foerster Photography; Page 14 © Snowleopard1; Page 15 © Fir0002, Nordelch; Page 16 © Steffen Foerster Photography, Gary & Sandy Wales; Page 17 © Stephen Meese; Page 18 © Karel Gallas; Page 19 © Galyna Andrushko, Bertrand Collet, Hywit Dimyadi, Fir0002, HTuller, Nordelch, Snowleopard, Johan Swanepoel, MONGO, Four Oaks, Kurt_G, Eric Gevaert, Steffen Foerster Photography, Gerrit_de_Vries, Steffen Foerster Photography, Margita, P.Uzunova, Galyna Andrushko, Galyna Andrushko, Bertrand Collet, Sebastian Kaulitzki; Page 20 © Jan Coetzee; Page 21 ©Yuri Arcurs; Page 22 © USDA ; Page 23 © Lee Torrens; Page 24 © MONGO, Jairo S. Feris Delgado; Page 25 © Unununium272, Brian Weed; Page 26 © Iñaki Antoñana Plaza; Page 28 © Robert Fullerton; Page 29 © Hannamariah

Editor: Jeanne Sturm

Cover and page design by Nicola Stratford, Blue Door Publishing

Library of Congress Cataloging-in-Publication Data

Lundgren, Julie K.
  Grassland buffet : studying food webs in the grasslands and savannahs / Julie K. Lundgren.
       p. cm. -- (Studying food webs)
  Includes index.
  ISBN 978-1-60472-318-2 (hardcover)
  ISBN 978-1-60472-783-8 (softcover)
  1. Grassland ecology--Juvenile literature. 2. Food chains (Ecology)--Juvenile literature. 3. Grasslands--Juvenile literature. I. Title.
  QH541.5.P7L86 2009
  577.4'16--dc22

Printed in the USA

CG/CG

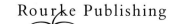

Rourke Publishing

www.rourkepublishing.com – rourke@rourkepublishing.com
Post Office Box 3328, Vero Beach, FL 32964

Table Of Contents

Chain of Foods   4

Grassland Buffet   8

Energy on the Move   18

A Clean Sweep   20

Broken Web   22

Glossary   30

Index   32

On The Cover

Wolf, a predator and top of the food chain. It preys on bison.

Bison, a herbivore, eats grass.

Grasses use sunlight to make food.

Sunlight, the beginning of a grassland food chain.

Chain of Foods

Earth's life depends on sunlight, food, water, and air. Through **photosynthesis**, green plants transform the Sun's light energy into food energy, a simple sugar they use to live and grow. Plant eaters take this energy and pass it on to meat eaters. The links showing the passage of energy form a **food chain**. Because organisms are links in many food chains, an area's food chains compose a **food web**.

CHEW On THIS

Photosynthesis requires water, carbon dioxide, and chlorophyll, a substance in green plants.

The Sun's energy moves through a food chain, beginning with green plants and ending with animals.

Grassland Connections

An **ecosystem** includes all of the plants and animals in an area and their relationships with each other and their surroundings. The climate and availability of resources, like water, food, and shelter, help determine the plant and animal species in an ecosystem. Grasslands are named different things

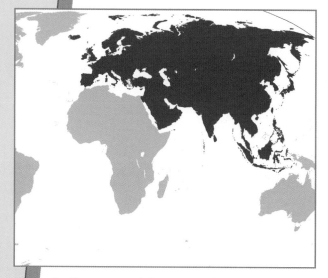

In Europe and Asia, grasslands are called steppes.

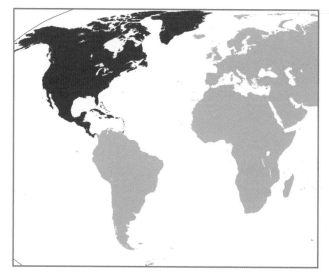

In North America, grasslands are called prairies.

in different places—like steppe, prairie, pampas, and savanna. Whatever the name, grasslands consist of flat, mostly treeless plains receiving 10 to 30 inches (25 to 75 cm) yearly rainfall. Any less rain produces deserts. More moisture results in forests.

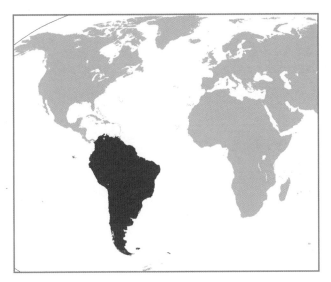

In South America, grasslands are called pampas.

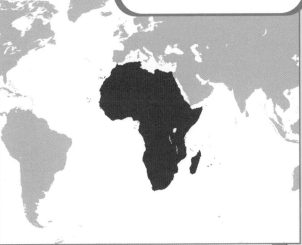

In Africa, grasslands are called savannas.

Grassland Buffet

Power Plants!

Green plants, the **primary producers**, make their own food. Primary means first. Primary producers are the first living things in food chains and form the ecosystem's food foundation. Many kinds of leafy grasses populate grasslands, but herbs and flowering plants, or forbs, outnumber grasses. Together, the seeds, roots, stems, leaves, berries, flowers, and nectar provide a vegetarian banquet.

CHEW ON THIS

Ecologists are scientists who study ecosystems.

Long, skinny leaves conserve water by exposing less surface to the Sun and wind.

Trees adapted to drought dot the savanna.

Rain, Wind, and Fire

Why don't trees take over grasslands? Three powerful elements maintain the landscape. First, wind constantly sucks moisture from plants. Second, dead plant material near the soil blocks most rain. Last, wildfires regularly consume the landscape. Grassland plant **adaptations** include deep root systems that gather water well. Also, plants go **dormant** during drought, sprouting again when conditions allow. Helpful fire burns invading tree seedlings and cleans out the thatch. Nutrients, sunlight, and rain can then reach the waiting roots.

Chinese Lanterns grow on the Eurasian steppe.

Long roots help grassland plants survive the powerful elements.

Silver pampas grasses shoot up to 12 feet (3.7 meters) high in the grasslands of South America.

Lassoing Lunch

Primary consumers, or herbivores, are the first animals in food chains. Adaptations enable these plant eaters to chew and digest tough grasses and seeds. In grasslands, grazing herbivores help keep woody plants like trees and shrubs from moving in. Grasses and forbs easily regenerate after animals trim them.

Many savanna herbivores feed on acacia tree leaves. Dik diks, small antelopes, nibble the lowest branches. Higher up, impalas munch.

Prairie dogs loosen the soil and trim the thatch.

Gerenuks, with the ability to stand on their rear legs, stretch up to the next level of leaves. Giraffes polish off all but the very highest leaves. Elephants hungry for acacia leaves topple the tree and pluck the remaining leaves. Each animal gets a share of food without wasting precious energy competing with other herbivores.

CHEW ON THIS

Nimble elephant trunks contain at least 40,000 different muscles.

After primary consumers come the **secondary consumers**. The animals at this level in the food chain eat the herbivores. Snakes, spiders, bats, members of the cat and dog families, and birds of prey all dine on other animals.

Black Mamba

Fearsome predators top food webs. Wolf packs use teamwork to hunt bison and elk. Cooperative hunting works for other carnivores, too. A wildebeest has only one chance in five of escaping a pack of African hunting dogs.

Omnivores aren't choosy at mealtime. Animals like foxes, coyotes, and jackals snap up insects, fruit, eggs, and meat.

Pangolins have strong front legs and claws, strong enough to tear into the mud castle homes of the termites they eat.

African hunting dogs kill large animals, like wildebeests.

Savanna Story

From leaping kudus, impalas, and springboks to galloping zebras, wildebeests, and Cape Horn buffalos, savanna herbivores provide predators a plentiful spread.

As a protection against predators, grazers often move and eat in herds. A large herbivore constantly watches for movement in the grass, signaling a hunter's presence. The herbivore must also lower its head to eat, and for a few moments, its eyes are on its food. During these moments the predator inches forward. Over several hours, the predator can get close enough to attempt a kill. In herds, however, many watch for danger. Also, a predator may lose sight of its target in the shifting movement of the herd. Zebra herds have perfected this distraction. With all those stripes, who can tell where one animal ends and another begins?

The ability to instantly leap away from predators makes impalas true fast food.

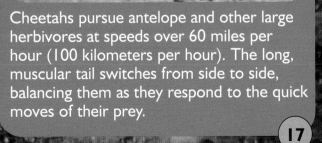

Cheetahs pursue antelope and other large herbivores at speeds over 60 miles per hour (100 kilometers per hour). The long, muscular tail switches from side to side, balancing them as they respond to the quick moves of their prey.

In Brazil, giant anteaters eat a slim diet of termites and ants. Anteaters save energy by sleeping 15 hours a day with their warm, bushy tails wrapped around them.

In a food web, a large foundation of producers supports the consumers with energy from the Sun. As energy is spent on its way to the top, fewer animals can be supplied with enough energy to meet their needs. Decomposers recycle food web waste from all food levels.

Top Predators
lions, hyenas, hunting dogs, eagles

Secondary Consumers (Carnivores and Omnivores)
pangolins, snakes, lizards, jackals, birds

Primary Consumers (Herbivores)
elephants, giraffes, insects, rodents, antelopes, wildebeests,

Primary Producers (Plants)

Decomposers
beetles, fungi, bacteria

Energy on the Move

Each food chain link represents an energy transfer as well as someone's dinner. Organisms both store and spend energy. They store energy in their bodies and spend energy taking care of daily functions. Organisms can only pass on the energy they've stored. As the energy moves up the food chain, the supply decreases. Predators eat many meals to meet their energy needs. So, ecosystems have many plants, some herbivores, and just a few top predators.

lions

hyenas, hunting dogs

eagles

pangolins

snakes, lizards

jackals

birds

elephants, giraffes

insects

rodents

antelopes, wildebeests, buffalo

leaves

fruit

nectar, flowers

grasses

beetles, fungi, bacteria

ENERGY FLOW

A Clean Sweep

Nature clears the table after plants and animals die. **Carrion** provides bargain dining for scavengers. No energy is spent in chasing it; all that's needed is a strong stomach! Then **decomposers** arrive. Earthworms, beetles, and millipedes join helpful microorganisms like fungi and soil bacteria in breaking down plant and animal waste into nutrients. The nutrients enter the food web again when plants slurp them up. Now that's recycling!

Spotted hyenas eat carrion in addition to hunting their own prey.

Microscopic bacteria number in the millions in a handful of soil.

Broken Web

People are part of food webs, too. Every action in our modern world has the potential of affecting food webs. How we get our energy—our food, our fuel—sometimes pulls the strands in the web to the breaking point.

Years of drought and poor farming practices caused the Dust Bowl in the North American prairie in the 1930s.

Rich, flat land attracts agriculture. Only fragments of the millions of acres of **native** grasslands in the United States still survive. Most farmers plant crops and add chemicals to enrich the soil and kill off weeds and pests. Chemicals not taken up by the plants pollute the environment. Plowed soil erodes without roots to hold it in place.

Huge machines efficiently harvest vast fields planted with one crop, such as wheat.

CHEW ON THIS

Grassland crops like corn and wheat feed much of the world's people.

ANIMALS IN DANGER!

Burrowing owls shelter underground, often in prairie dog tunnels. Pesticides and plows affect habitat used by burrowing owls.

On the Asian steppe, a species of wild horse called Przewalski's horses nearly died out because of grazing cattle.

Warming Up

Earth's temperature is rising. Caused mainly by greenhouse gases like carbon dioxide, global warming affects all of Earth's ecosystems. When fossil fuels like coal, oil, and natural gas burn, they release carbon dioxide. Carbon dioxide in the atmosphere acts like a greenhouse, trapping heat. It keeps the planet's temperature warm enough to support life. When the atmosphere holds too much carbon dioxide, Earth's climate changes.

Cheetahs had a population of about 100,000 in 1900. Only 12,000 to 15,000 exist in the wild today, mainly due to illegal hunting.

Americans own 33 percent of the world's cars yet make up less than 5 percent of Earth's population.

Patching a Web

Everyone can help bring Earth back into balance by practicing good **stewardship**. Taking care of the world for the sake of future generations requires a reduction in energy consumption. Moving to clean energy like solar and wind power is key to reducing fossil fuel use. Carpooling, taking the bus, and turning down the heat are all ways to save energy.

CHEW ON THIS

Though wind farms provide green fuel, ecologists wonder if they disturb nesting birds like lesser prairie-chickens.

Garbage mounts in landfills. Recycling paper, metals, plastic, and motor oil means energy savings and less mining and trash. Many store products are wrapped in huge amounts of unnecessary packaging. Wise shoppers choose products with little or no packaging, products made from recycled wood, paper, or plastic, and items that come in recyclable containers.

CHEW ON THIS

Environmental groups and governments encourage manufacturers to achieve zero landfill status. Factories reuse or recycle all manufacturing waste, and save money, too.

Where tallgrass prairie once grew, individuals, companies, schools, and governments have set aside land for prairie restoration. Restoration means bringing something back to its original condition. In prairie restoration, crops and weeds are removed. Then, workers plant native grasses and forbs. Every few years, controlled fires renew restored prairies as wildfires did in days of old. Still, prairie managers know the original prairies had many more plants and animals than the rebuilt prairies.

A fire specialist watches over a controlled burn.

Restored prairies allow people to appreciate firsthand the beauty and ecology of grasslands. Quality of life, convenience, and comforts must be balanced with the needs of ecosystems. Scientists and educators teamed with governments, the media, and manufacturers can make a difference. So, too, can individuals. As people come to understand the need for change, balance will return, and with it, a healthier planet.

Glossary

adaptations (ad-ap-TAY-shunz): ways of survival that animals and plants have to be successful in their environment

carrion (KAIR-ee-yon): bodies of dead animals

decomposers (dee-cum-POH-zerz): animals and plants that cause rot and decay, enriching the soil with valuable nutrients

dormant (DOR-muhnt): a state of inactivity

ecosystem (EE-koh-sis-tum): the relationships between all the plants and animals and the place in which they live

food chain (FOOD CHAYN): a series of plants and animals, each of which is eaten by the one after it

food web (FOOD WEHB): in an ecosystem, the intricate network of food chains

native (NAY-tiv): naturally occurring, living in the place where it originated

omnivores (AHM-nih-vorz): animals that feed on a wide variety of foods including both plants and animals

photosynthesis (foh-toh-SIN-thuh-siss): the process by which green plants transform the Sun's energy into food

primary consumers (PRYE-mair-ee kahn-SOO-merz): herbivores, the animals that eat primary producers

primary producers (PRYE-mair-ee proh-DOO-serz): plants that perform photosynthesis

secondary consumers (SEHK-uhn-dair-ee kahn-SOO-merz): animals that eat herbivores

stewardship (STU-werd-ship): responsibility for taking care of something not owned

Further Reading

Hungry for more? Your local library serves up additional information about grassland ecology and food webs. Whet your appetite with these books and websites.

Books

Allaby, Michael. *Grasslands*. Chelsea House, 2006.

Lynch, Wayne. *Prairie Grasslands*. NorthWord Books for
    Young Readers, 2006.

Johnson, Kirk. *Gas Trees and Car Turds: A Kids' Guide to the Roots of
    Global Warming*. Fulcrum Publishing, 2007.

Websites

Neal Smith National Wildlife Refuge
www.tallgrass.org

EEK! Environmental Education for Kids
www.dnr.state.wi.us/eek/

Bell Museum of Natural History: Build-A-Prairie
www.bellmuseum.org/distancelearning/prairie/build/

Index

Africa   7, 15
carbon dioxide   4, 25
carnivore   15, 18
climate   6, 25
decomposers   18, 20, 22
ecosystem(s)   6, 8, 18, 25, 29
global warming   25
herbivore(s)   12, 13, 14, 16, 17, 18
microorganisms   20
North America   6, 22
pampas   7, 11

photosynthesis   4
prairie(s)   6, 29
predator(s)   15, 16, 18
prey   14, 17, 20
primary consumers   12, 14, 18
primary producers   8, 18
savanna   7, 9, 12, 16
secondary consumers   14, 18
steppe   6, 7, 10, 24
stewardship   26

About the Author

Julie K. Lundgren grew up near Lake Superior where she reveled in mucking about in the woods, picking berries, and expanding her rock collection. Her appetite for learning about the intricate details of nature led her to a degree in biology from the University of Minnesota. She currently lives in Minnesota with her husband and two sons.